MIRABILIA

Also by Lisa Gorton

Press Release
Hotel Hyperion
The Best Australian Poems 2013 (ed.)
The Life of Houses
Empirical

LISA GORTON

MIRABILIA

NEW POEMS

First published 2022
from the Writing and Society Research Centre
at Western Sydney University
by the Giramondo Publishing Company
PO Box 752
Artarmon NSW 1570 Australia
www.giramondopublishing.com

Cover and design by Jenny Grigg
Typesetting by Andrew Davies
in 9/15 pt Tiempos Regular

Printed and bound by Ligare Book Printers
Distributed in Australia by NewSouth Books

A catalogue record for this
book is available from the
National Library of Australia.

ISBN: 978-1-922725-30-1

The Giramondo Publishing Company acknowledges the support of Western Sydney University in the implementation of its book publishing program.

This project has been assisted by the Commonwealth Government through the Australia Council, its arts funding and advisory body.

For my mother

What does it mean to say
We said something?
Bertolt Brecht

Contents

Muse

Mirabilia

if that which is at all were not forever
Marianne Moore, 'The Pangolin'

It is its

own order—scaled mammal that can

spiral itself in

armour safe in the lion's jaws—

it is toothless, its

belly is naked,

its only predator is man—

Adept alike of

dry savanna and equatorial canopies

it walks on riverbeds—Huyghen van Linschoten, a

Dutchman in Goa,

when fishers hauled one out, thought it

a strange fish—

it being middle-sized-dog-sized,

elephant-footed,

snorting like a hog—

its head tail legs all cased in scales

        harder than iron

or steel—

        Mild moving anvil,

they hewed at it with weapons—and

it rolled up

and could not be prised open—its

picture, for a wonder, they sent to the King of Spain—

In the pouch of its eyelid its

near-blind round black eye has written

underneath—

I

have seen it—

It goes by smell, its

        way of going—through

the vast plain-like stretches or dank

leaf mould straight up trees—

could solve the problem
of depicting a mind thinking so that the idea
is not separate from the act
of experiencing it—
imagined mind that goes subtly
reasoning forwards
on an unforseen line surely
to the place—
When it
comes to it, it goes
nose shut ears shut eyes shut headfirst
into what it likes—
it bathes in ants, it
is particular—
wries its tongue (free-drawn
line out
from its snout's blunted pencil tip)
against a wrong taste—

It goes on hind legs—its finger-

    length-clawed hands it folds

one over another or at

    times taps down—it can

carve concrete—

Its tail its counterweight it holds

    with hoop-skirt-like up-

rightness

    (yearly with raw silk

pink pinking-shear-trimmed

    pangopup bustle)

under which its legs go with a

    separate light ease

unexpected under armour—

its armour is not put on—the

    snake's head helmet be-

tween its eyes at its nape outspreads

in overlapping scallop-shell-ridged scales of ochre,

amber, olive-brown

each edged with lighter bands

so when it goes—with

wave-through-wave

movement along a branch or in

night grasslands as one

unbroken wave—its repeating

varied scales track light

like a principle of growth—each

one replacing each

other's vanishing—as if that which is could be for-

ever—

It is toothless, its

belly is naked—

its only predator is man—

The Replica (2020)

This is the beginning of the replica.
A memorial or archetype. It is to be
kept under glass in Council Offices
perpetually. It is still being made—
houses trees parks towers windows
reticulated by a grid of trenches
visible from space. It is a receptacle.
Its air, the substance of its distances,
can be drawn on, struck with a bell,
or carved into star shapes and cubes
in which its flaws, or side-lit baubles,
at once hang in stillness and sheer
off—Night and day the weather plays
over it. Its dome shifts the light
a little to one side and where its streets
run up against the barricades its glass

is handpainted with clouds of snow-

covered peaks—or they might be islands

afloat at the end of the sea. This is

the beginning of the replica. A memorial

or archetype. It is still being made.

On the Characterisation of Male Poets' Mothers

I

Charles Baudelaire's mother—

orphaned at seven—living

on the charity of friends—

at twenty-six married

an ex-priest, widower—

After her husband died she married again

and was happy—

It is said— 'This second marriage

was to have a disastrous effect on his life'—

'No longer being the sole focus

of his mother's attention gave him a trauma'—

'When you have a son like me

you do not remarry'—

He asked her endlessly for money—

She repaid his publishers—

He wrote to her—

> ‘I am the only object which makes you live’—
>
> ‘After my death, you will no longer live, that’s clear’—
>
> He wrote repeatedly of returning to Honfleur—
>
> He passed through there once by train
>
> and did not stop—

II

Rainer Maria Rilke's mother—

whose first child died at two weeks—

it is said— 'acted as if she sought to recover the lost girl

through the boy

by dressing him in girl's clothing'—

and hurt her husband's 'sensibilities'

by 'parading the boy in female dress'—

Victoria and Albert Museum of Childhood—

'In Western European countries until about 1920

boys would wear dresses until they were "breeched"—

"breeching" happened from the age of about four-

to eight-years-old'—

She gave him the doll, doll-bed and kitchen that he wanted—

He spent hours combing his doll's hair—

He had a 'sabre hammered in gold', a knight's 'tin decoration'—

He was, he wrote, 'eating like a wolf, sleeping like a sack'—

When he turned six she breeched him and took him to school—

He suffered from headaches and fevers—

She sat by his bed, through all the hours, to soothe him—

    In his second year of primary school, two-hundred hours—

    In his third year of primary school, two whole quarters—

His father left—The grandparents were no help—

His father blamed his mother for his unhappiness

    at the military school

    which his father had chosen—

He wrote to her almost every day—

He wanted letters, food packets, skates, visits—

She gave him these—

Whenever she left—they say—he felt abandoned—

‘If in my father’s house’

(his father had left)

‘love was shown me with both care and concern only by my father’

(he lived with his mother)

‘you know those persons who are to blame—

and that the woman whose first and most immediate care

I should have been

loved me only when bringing me out in a new little dress’—

‘Quiet endurance and courageous resignation,’

he said, were his thing—

his suffering, ‘only the whim

of a pitiful, pleasure-seeking creature (Mother)’—

III

Arthur Rimbaud's mother—

according to reports—

was 'sour-faced'—

was 'narrow-minded, stingy,

completely lacking in a sense of humour'—

was 'renfermée, têtue et taciturne'—

He named her his 'Mouth of Darkness'—

His father—

'good-natured, easygoing, generous'—

came home on leave only to give her another child—

Ten weeks with her—five children—

after which he did not come back again—

When the youngest was four he retired

easily to Dijon—

She named herself a widow—

She worried about the children's education—

She had to call the police to bring him home—

In Paris, he put sulphuric acid into Charles Cros's water—

He stabbed a knife into Verlaine's wrist—

His 'teen rebel phase', they say, was 'a reaction to life with Vitalie'—

He stayed with her all summer writing 'A Season in Hell'—

She paid for it to be published—

When she asked him what it meant he answered

'It means what it says'—

From Africa, he kept writing her letters—

he wanted books, goods—he had tasks for her—

He had 'a romantic view of his father'—

‘My dear Mummy—

I got your letter and the two stockings alright—

Do not be upset about all this, however—

But it’s a poor reward for so much work—

so many privations and troubles—

P.S. As for the stockings, they are useless—I shall sell them

somewhere’—

In 1890, a photo—she stands in her garden with flowers—

IV

Philip Larkin's mother

sent him 'seven enormous pairs of socks'

and lilies to brighten up his room—

'Dear Creaturely Mop, this seems a good time to warn you

I am down to my last three pounds'—

She wrote to him—

'Marriage would be no certain guarantee

as to socks being always mended,

or meals ready when they are wanted.

Neither would it be a good idea to marry

just for these comforts. There are other things

just as important'—

for which, she has been held responsible for his not marrying—

'He couldn't marry anyone

because he was involved with his mother'—

It is said— she was 'nervous, constantly whining'—

'she was the poet's muse—and his millstone'—

She wrote— 'When I came to the sketch of me,

I laughed outright'—

His father attended Nazi rallies—

In his mother, though, he complained of

'a kind of "defective mechanism". Her ideal is

"to collapse" and to be taken care of'—

'Dear Mop Creature—send some underclothes please'—

The Book of Revelations

Photograph, 1952: 'Untitled (Cynthia Nolan with Parasol
            Mounted on Dead Horse)'

She smiles.

The horse has eyeless sockets—
    crows plucked them out.
Its face is eaten half away.
They have saddled it—
    pulled a bridle with snare bit over its crumbled ear.
Under the saddle its left side gapes—
    stripped bone cage—
its chest rent where dogs and lizards
    got at its heart.

'Blessing, and honour, and glory, and power'—

She has clambered onto a dead thing

propped in its litter of bones—

She smiles.

The artist said—

'Death takes on a curiously abstract pattern

under these arid conditions'—

The artist strung the carcass of a dead calf in a tree—

I think I know that smile.

A cypher on the face of self-illiterate rage.

Ashamed of what they've asked. Accommodating.

Speech of the dust.

'And I saw, & behold a white horse: and he that sat on him

had a bow; and a crown was given unto him'—

On one side of her, Brian the Stockman props the dead horse up.

On the other, a woman (unnamed) reaches a hand out

    to fix the bridle against its long jawbone—

She smiles.

'And lo a black horse; and he that sat on him

    had a pair of balances in his hand'—

The artist had a pocket microscope.

The artist had an Agfa camera with a monocular lens.

The artist had binoculars turned front to back

    to see things afloat in a sea of glass.

The artist had trained his eye to open and look and shut

    and turn away.

They were at Wave Hill, on Vestey Station—

‘And the kings of the earth—

And the great men—

And the rich men—

And the chief captains—

And the mighty men—

And the bondmen—

And every free man’—

where families living on the dry river bed

got paid in tins of jam.

In her right hand she holds an umbrella

raised to shade her face.

The artist had painted ‘Daisy Bates at Ooldea’—

a dead thing floating in a landscape—

umbrella in her right hand—her mouth

is painted out.

These carcasses—the artist said—are
    ‘preserved in strange shapes which have often
    a kind of beauty, or grim elegance’—

The artist moved their skulls and bones about—
    stacked carcasses one on another—
    set one on its back with its legs in the air—
propped the dead horse on its hind legs with its
    mouth in the dust.

I think I know that smile.

Ekphrasis. The Nymph of Fontainebleau

A bronze relief for a king—

a spring personified—

a nymph stretched out between the hounds and prey

drinking from the goddess—

'You know that poor young girl Caterina—

I keep her principally for my art's sake—

but being a man also

I have used her for my pleasure'—

'Cellini carved a firm,

slender,

supple body

in accordance with the Mannerist canon—

With this elongated,

lissom,

naked body

he carved a veritable ode

to feminine beauty'—

'And it is possible that she may bear me a child—

Now I do not want to maintain

another man's bastard—

Accordingly, dear brother, I entreat you

to be my helper'—

'Cellini's characteristic style is easily recognisable—

The mouth accentuated

by a clear line beneath it—

the lower lip curved in the middle—

the dilated pupils—

the manner in which the eyelids are drawn—

tiny stripes

indicating the hairs of the eyebrows'—

'I returned to my castle where I all but caught

Pagolo and that little wench Caterina—

advancing, not knowing what they said—

nor, like people in a trance, where they were going—

Not content with having made him take

that vicious drab for a wife,

I completed my revenge by hiring her again—

I made her pose before me naked—I made her

serve my pleasure out of spite against her husband

jeering at them both the while—

I kept her hours together in unnatural poses—

This gave her as much hurt

as it gave me pleasure for she was beautifully made'—

'Its extreme elongation—

precariously balanced pose—is

typical of Mannerist sculpture'—

'The second time Caterina spoke of her husband
I seized her by the hair and dragged her up and down
beating and kicking her till I was tired—
There was no one who could come to help her—
When I saw her body
torn and bruised and swollen I reflected that—
even if I could persuade her to return—
I'd have to put her under medical treatment
for at least a fortnight
before I could make use of her'—

'The austere beauty of the face
recalls antique sculpture'—
'tight parallel folds of drapery and volutes
representing water
set off the smooth modelling of the flesh'—

‘In contrast to his idealized view

of the female body,

the sculptor treats the animals in a naturalistic manner’—

Tongue

One unhappy day I was called to see
the Benois Madonna—
I found myself confronted by a young woman
with a bald forehead and puffed cheeks,
a toothless smile, blear eyes, and a furrowed throat—
And yet I had to acknowledge
that this painful affair was the work of Leonardo da Vinci.
It was hard, but the effort freed me,
and the indignation I felt
gave me the resolution to proclaim my freedom—
Bernard Berenson

Tongue

—bre 1478 I began the two Virgin Marys
Leonardo Da Vinci

The Madonna of the Flowers has a line

of black behind her teeth—The tongue

in its dark laps air—'and by that the sounding

out of all the names of things is'—

On her lap the child is catching at the pale

flowers in her hand raised now into the light

of that bare window cut through stone

at the back filled with nothing but sky—

its lead-white thinly over black—Flowers

of the cross, cruciferae, bittercress—the child's

hand is black along its knuckles where it

reaches to catch those pale flowers foreshadowing

death his mother hands to him—*first*

begotten of the dead—his dying already growing

through his hand's flesh—'When you begin

the hand from within first separate all the bones
a little'—Young Lorenzo di Credi in his
imitation had the child take an acorn *righteousness*
out of his mother's hand—the child's hand
of a corpse in the still light of that soundless room
where the window has a city in it and in the corner
her bed is made—'When I made a Christ Child
you put me in prison'—Its stained walls, patterns
of joined stone—a landscape complete with
mountains, battles, faces, clouds—'A thing miraculous'—
its blank surface opening into a window of dawn
light that is touchable, originary—'The sun has never
seen a shadow'—A stone room held between
that light and this—a watcher standing in the doorway
in the place of light that casts its shadow back
across her mouth, her ear, the child's right hand, right foot—
marking on them *the lamb of the trespass offering*—
blood where its shadows are—as that metal driven

through her ear means *I will not go out free*—A window of sky
in the shape of a diptych which will be painted in—
a Pietà, a child tearing flowers—'The first drawing
was the outline of a shadow'—Now these figures
'clothed in light and darkness' round forwards
into the light of its window reversed—history, prophecy
meeting in its stone room—At the crossing place
her gem—like water closed in glass—holds light
where in opaque things light's shadows are and is
indifferent, afloat inside its curve, lit against
and leashed to any watcher's eye—incloses
a room above their turning hands—a nearly
conceivable place in which the doorway's reflection
invents what could be a window at the back
where its two shadows wait and its bittercress
changes into pale points of light—a single pearl there
making the *palle*—its heraldry hung upon abyss—
how such lustres move to meet and equal always

the distance of any watcher's eye, its unassimilable

contrary and end—Encircling it the fifteen pearls

of her suffering are to be counted over repeatedly—

blood in her mouth—the tongue in its dark laps air—

Madonna of the Flowers

Easter Sunday, 1478—

the one they called Fioretta—

'little flower'—

her child one month old

and the child's father—

they called him

'Prince of Youth'—

was stabbed at Mass

in the Cathedral of Saint Mary

of the Flowers—

lily and bittercress—

stabbed nineteen times—

dying at the altar

of San Zanobi, saint of the child

brought back to life—a child five years old

lost in the marketplace,

broken under the oxcart's

wheel and doubled,

afloat in bronze relief

on the saint's box shrine—

They had dug up

the relics—

had Cione make 'a head

of silver to contain

a piece of the head of that Saint'

to be carried on feast days

through the streets—

flowers

on the tower where he

once lived—

His ring they sent

for a cure

to the King of France—

This Fioretta, fifteen years old—

Varchi says,

the daughter of an armourer—

one Antonio di Michele

del Ciptadino

who made corazze

in the Borgo Pinti—

and Giuliano de' Medici

wore no corazza

to the church that day—

his murderers,

fetching him to Mass, jesting

that he was growing fat,

caressed his waist to check—

not the corazza

'covered with peacock velvet'—

not the corazza

'covered in green silk velvet'

in his armoury—its heaped shields,

swords, lances—

its corazza all'antica of silver—

naked metal body

that he dressed in

on the day of his giostra—

empty sculpture fronted

with Medusa's mask—

her mouth wide open, tongue

lapped out—

And Fioretta's given name

was Antonia—

was Antonietta—

and she gave birth in a stone room

in Borgo Pinti

and Antonio da Sangallo

lived across the street—

his brother Giuliano had been

six years building a house there

for the Chancellor Scala

'dei bell'inchini'—his coat of arms

a ladder

on a field of gold—

and Giuliano de' Medici—

'Prince of Youth'—

had set the price

of the first land

Scala bought in Borgo Pinti—

Mona Piera's house and garden

with its apple orchards

and its vines—

land belonging to

the Ospedale degli Innocenti—

'*rifugio di miserie e di colpe*'—its *Nocentini* named Ignoti

Poverelli

Esposito

Innocenti

Trovato

to be found again by a sign—

a half-coin

a cut ribbon

a broken medal

five hundred florins to be paid in full

when the widow died—

Scala promising the dowry

for a girl to be married

ASF *Notarile* M 530, fols. 3r-9r, *passim* (1470)

to a servant of the Signoria—

and the Prince of Youth's tutor,

hating Scala, said—*safe in his pomerium*

by the walls this madman

rich from public embezzlement

takes his ease

among obscene wolves,

not to call them something worse—

Fioretta, Antonia—

'a free woman'—

and they sent Antonio da Sangallo

to tell *Il Magnifico* Lorenzo

who wanted

no news of the child—

his dead brother

having been promised

to Semiramide d'Appiani d'Aragona,

daughter

of the lord of Piombino,

ally of Naples—

and the king of Naples

and the pope in league

were making war on Florence

saying, 'Lorenzo de' Medici alone

of all the Florentines

they held for an enemy'—

excommunicating the city—

besieging Castellina—

Only *Il Magnifico's* mother—

who had tried to climb

into her dead son's coffin—he was buried at last

on the Feast of the Ascension—

said she would not

give up the child—

so *Il Magnifico*—

going to the place

where Fioretta was—

taking the child from her—

handed her child

into Antonio's care

until his seventh year—

and they baptised him—three days after the Feast

of San Zanobi,

a month to the day

after his father died—

and Antonio held her child

at baptism

'in memory of Giuliano'—

and they named him—*firstborn of the dead*—

'Giulio & Zanobi

di Giuliano di Piero'—

[mother unnamed in the register—]

and Fioretta died that year,

they said—or,

she went into a nunnery—

and Scala bought cheap land

where the pillaging armies had been—

The Pazzi Conspiracy Medal:
Giuliano Murdered
Reverse: Lorenzo Escapes The Assassins

That afternoon *Il Magnifico* stood in the window of his palace, a bandage at his throat, clothes stained with blood—said, 'Do not harm the innocent'—They had thrown the conspirators from the high windows of the Signoria—left them to hang—the mercenaries they killed inside the building—bodies stripped naked, hacked apart—now a head fixed on a spear—torso on a sword-tip—to be carried through the streets—'so many deaths that the streets were filled with the parts of men'—dead bodies propped inside the windows of the notaries—'naked as the day they were born'—and they looked 'like men created to look alive'—like those effigies Verrocchio made with Orsino the waxworker—skeletons of wood bodied with woven reed—flesh of waxed cloth, folded—head, hands and feet of wax cast from life and painted wet on wet—'so life-like that they seemed no images in wax but living men'—and one they dressed in the blood-stained clothes that *Il Magnifico* wore that day—propped by the miraculous crucifix of the Chiarita where once San Zanobi healed a rich man of his sore throat—and one they dressed in his *lucco,* inside the door of *Santa Annunziata,* kneeling by the place where candles are sold—its bodies on horseback, bodies in armour, bodies strung from ropes—its hands of wax and eyes, ears, teeth, arms—and chains of silver—chains of iron—brides came to leave their flowers there where once an angel painted the virgin's likeness while a painter slept in despair of imagining the beauty of her face—and they paid Orsino the waxworker twelve fiorini—and the two boy choristers in the train of Cardinal Riario, crossing the square to the palace, were torn apart by the crowd—

Istoria

after Poliziano

All that month, rain—

Cavaliere Giacopo was caught in the hills of the Faltero

and though he offered his captors gold to kill him there

they hauled him back to Florence, sold him for fifty florins

at the city gate—he was hanged from the Signoria, buried

with the noose around his neck in the Pazzi crypt—

Unseasonable rain, and the harvest spoiling—

they crowded into the city, said his burial had ruined

the grain and milk—and the friars of Santa Croce dug up

his three-week corpse, carted it to unconsecrated ground

by the Gate of Justice leading to the gallows—

And the rain stopped—Still they heard strange sounds

in that place—and a throng of boys dug up the corpse again,

dragged it by its noose through the city streets—heralds

sent before them to cry 'the great knight'—and they dragged

the corpse to its palazzo, knocked its head against the door—

'Who's there?

Who's inside?

Is there no one to receive the master

returning with his retinue?'

Sketch

29 December, 1479—

The artist stood in the street, sketching—

'A tan-coloured small cap

A doublet of black serge

A black jerkin, lined, and the collar covered with black

and red stippled velvet

A blue coat lined with fur of foxes' breasts

Black hose

Bernardo di Bandino Baroncelli'—

hanged, together with his wife, from a window of the Palazzo

del Capitano—

[his wife not in the picture]

Medusa's Mask

Then was the iron, the clay, the brass, the silver,
and the gold, broken to pieces together—
Daniel, 2:35

In the workshop of Verrocchio—

In the city of dead bodies—In the year

of the wars, in the year of the plague

[Otto]bre 1478—I began the two Virgin Marys—

No attendant angels—mother and child

alone. A stone room with a window in it.

A mouthful of shadow. A name.

A poor flower, bittercress—four petals

for the cross. A fold of skin at her neck

where the milk rises—

the child seven months old—in the house

of Antonio, maker of engines—her child

in his care until the seventh year—

A half-coin. A cut ribbon. A broken medal—

They paid their Botticelli forty gold florins

to paint a *pittura infamante* on the wall

over the Customs Gate—

dead men hanging from a window

upside down in chains—

Alberti writing of the painted dead—

everything hangs—hands, fingers and head—

everything falls—the painting of the dead

should be dead to the very nails—

its shadow on the child's hand, shadow in her mouth—

Now on a wall marked with stains I see

the faces of men—*as in the clamour of bells*

I can hear any name I choose—

Their Botticelli's bloodless glamour—they

admire it—have him make the dead

man's likeness from the death-

mask of his face—waxed cloth in its

stab wounds—propping the body in that narrow

room between the picture frame and its

window at the back—of touchable light—

recalling those bodies in the windows

of the notaries—in the window of my father

the notary—like effigies but they darken—

those effigies Verrocchio made with Orsino
the waxworker—taking the mask of *Il Magnifico*
to make his likeness in clay—exact

even to the eyelashes, the pricked pores of his face—
a dead thing—its clay
packed on iron rods, nails and twisted wire—

Write down what the soul is—

Not three years since I worked with Verrocchio
to make the Prince of Youth's likeness in clay—
silver armour in clay, clay Medusa's mask—

her mouth in shadow, tongue lapped out—
she was raped in the shrine—for this the shining-
eyed goddess taught Perseus to see her

only in a mirror—or shield of polished steel—

he killed her while she was sleeping—her eyes

turned living things to stone—*she had* *Ariosto*

a thousand lidless eyes that she could never close—

a likeness he kept in his room—his

opposite and double—kept propped on it

the golden helmet that we made

for the day of his giostra—a prize

they gave—a sallet in the shape of a cut-off

lion's head—copper gilt on steel—

its mane like water doubling back on itself—

its eyes black semi-precious stone—

its mouth red painted steel—living eyes

looked from the shadow of the lion's mouth—

on the day of his giostra—when *the surface* *Anonymous record*
of his shield was filled by a Medusa-head out-
lined in pearls, eleven ounces of them, scattered—

Now Verrocchio—sitting at his table heaped
with hands, limbs, heads, all cast from life out of
the soft stone of Volterra and Sienna

burned, crushed and mixed to paste—has buyers
setting the heads of their dead over the doors
and windows of their living places—

Who's there?

Who's inside?

putting me in mind to make *a picture in oils*

of the head of a Medusa—this picture being *Vasari*

round—a shield of Perseus

with her sleeping image afloat in its

abyss—its single instant in which she

sees herself seeing herself—her

mouth in shadow, tongue lapped out—

death in its mirror, stone—a stopped

face in its coil of living snakes—

A mouthful of shadow. A name.

Magnificence

In his study *Il Magnifico* kept a bronze statue of Marsyas
they called *The Nude of Fear.* He liked to think about
the mechanics of clocks. He had Verrocchio finish his
antique porphyry statue of Marsyas, its missing limbs made
with such art they had white veins in the red stone
where nerves show in living bodies when they are flayed.
Among his treasures he kept a mirrored glass sphere,
a unicorn's horn the length of a lance, an elephant's tooth.
When he adopted the child he made out the mother
had been 'a woman of the Gorini, his friend'. After he died
they found his doctor drowned upside down in a well.

Great World Atlas

for Izabela Pluta

Map

Black velvet, a curtain spread across a table on the footpath part in a Moreton Bay fig tree's unstill shade, folds heavily over thc concrete, the fleshy ridges of the tree roots shouldering out of its cut-out square of dirt—A single white balloon tied to the metal gate beats repeatedly against the stone head carved into the gatepost—its two faces a lock of stone hair falls between, stone eyes abyss looks through—Through the broken gate into the garden, its sunlit rectangle of grass, a woman sits reading—Her book is folio, hardcover, covers her face—the cover has a globe on it, golden, a ball in a net—Her chair, at the centre of the garden, is on a Persian rug, its inner field crimson with dark blue crosses inside repeating squares—Late summer, late afternoon, over the woman the sky is filmy—the white blinds are closed in the high terrace houses along the ridge, the last with walled stairs down to where the street goes steeply to the sea—The woman, closing the book, reveals at her side a girl stooped over a side table, rolling a peeled apple over a silver tray—its juice a clouded silver—Avidly the flies, flaring before her hand, cluster back upon its shining plain—Outside, this side of the wall, a young woman is walking down to the sea—her dress is wide, summer flowers on blue-green ground—Her shadow, separating from the tree's shadow, passing like a wave over the black-velvet-covered table, uncovers its instruments, each with its price sticker—a telescope, a stereoscope, a rangefinder camera, which, when she looks through it at the garden, turning its calibrated wheel, has bee-thick wisteria pendant from the iron lace entwining with the vine leaves enchased on the silver tray—the rug's grid of crosses extending across the grass—the child now with a glass-eyed doll hugged in her arms—In the carousel the slides are upside down and backwards—She slides a coral island, complete with palm trees, across the footpath—It swells over and shrinks into the folds of the tree roots, accommodating the tree's ridged bark, a sea now darkening with scratches—now distant mountains of bare rock—blue-shadowed glaciers—salt flats widening out to shadow-hills—where now a yellow-black blotch transforms into a sky column, light through cloud—She stands turning the landscapes over in her hands—Overhead, invisibly from below, a map is forming, its lines the colour of a scratch in glass—Suspended at first over the table, exactly to scale, marking each object's outline, it begins drawing upwards at the pace at which the shadow of the ridge is sliding sideways, filling the fig tree's unstill shade in with its single darkness—the camera now vanishing into the table—the table into the garden—the street into the city—the city into a single point.

The Reader's Digest Great World Atlas 1961 (1962)

Between the time of its publication and fourth revise they exploded the bomb they called Vanya over Novaya Zemlya—its fireball five miles wide hung a second sun over the island—its cloud rose into the mesosphere—black rain over the Kara Sea, Barents Sea, Alaska, Norway, Finland, Ukraine, northern Canada—lines leading back to the closed cities—to Arzamas-16 (Sarov), to Chelyabinsk-70 (Snezhinsk), near the Mayak site where they loosed the radioactive waste into Lake Karachay, Lake Irtyash, into the Techa river, past the villages, to the Arctic Sea—its radioactive cloud moving northeast over Berydanish, Satlykovo, out to Tygish—Between the time of its publication and fourth revise they exploded the bomb they called Starfish Prime off Johnston Atoll over French Frigate Shoals, high inside the thermosphere—Its aurora—a blinding white flash, green sphere of light, vast cloud outflung in turning arcs, in circles sweeping outwards—flared across the earth's magnetic field lines, debris lighting the sky from Taraw, on the equator, down to Apia, Wellington, Tongatapu, Campbell Island—trapping radiation along the field lines, irradiating the satellites TELSTAR, KOSMOS, ARIEL—the classified 'national reconnaissance satellites' ZENIT, CORONA, gridding the earth in rectangles of film—Its fallout rained over the world—Between the time of its publication and fourth revise they exploded plutonium over the saltbush scrub of Maralinga, at Taranaki, north of the straight train line across the Nullarbor, in secret trials they had named Operation Tims and Operation Vixen—its plumes, a hundred miles long, drifted on the wind—They had taken the sacred objects, trucked the people south across the rail line to the coast at Yalata—She said, 'Where are we going? We are going to a place we have never been to'—Some people walked, leaving sand tracks in the desert for the people left behind—lines leading back to Calder Hall at Windscale on the grey Irish Sea—Between the time of its first publication and fourth revise they exploded the bomb they called Storax Sedan underground at the Nevada Test Site, as part of their Peaceful Nuclear Explosions program, lifting a dome of earth ninety metres above the desert floor—more than twelve million tonnes of earth exploding outwards, a radioactive cloud separating into two, drifting northeast and then east over Iowa, Nebraska, South Dakota, Illinois, across to the Atlantic—In Las Vegas people watched the explosions at the Test Site from their hotel windows, put on their radiation badges and sat outside—its clouds spreading between the Cascade and Rocky Mountain Ranges—They collected the children's teeth for a study—Between the time of its publication and fourth revise they exploded the bomb they called Bighorn over Christmas Island (Kiritimati) in their yearlong Dominic series of thirty-one nuclear explosions over the 'Pacific Proving Ground'—filmed with EG&G Inc. rapatronic cameras, at 2400 frames a second, at one frame a minute—capturing its fireball, sun-like until its shockwave, rebounding off the ground, smashed into it, a cloud—a film-like sequence of high-speed photographs—'the critical information needed to build better bombs'—lines leading back to Los Alamos, to the Lawrence Livermore National Laboratory, to Hanford in sage-bush country on the Columbia River—Between the time of its first publication and fourth revise they exploded more than a hundred atmospheric bombs at the Semipalatinsk Test Site (the Polygon) in Kazakhstan, south of the valley of the River Irtysh, out to the Karagandy Ranges, south as far as Degelen Mountain, east to Chagan, where the river bends—testing them on purpose-built apartments, bridges, underground metro stations, trucks, planes—black winds over the industrial city of Ust-Kamenogorsk, Znamenka and the Kazakh Steppe, the towns and villages—at Dispensary No. 4 (IRME) they studied its effects on the local people and their newborn children—She said, 'Like hair burning—the smell came back from the earth each time it rained'—Between the time of its first publication and fourth revise they fired the thermonuclear warhead they called Operation K from Kapustin Yar south of Stalingrad (Volgograd) towards the Sary Shagan test range, detonating it in the troposphere southwest of Zhezqazghan—a pulse so strong it fused buried power cables for six-hundred miles—Between the time of its first publication and fourth revise they exploded the fourth of their Gerboise bombs over Reggane's 'Sahara Centre for Military Experiments'—a vast flash, an enormous ball of bluish fire, red at its centre, a cloud carried on the desert wind—That same year, they started on their nuclear test series with jewel names in the granite mountains at In Eker—the desert base they named Oasis 2, invisible from the road, east of Tan Afella—where during Operation Béryl the steel door of the tunnels exploded into the air on a rush of flame—its ochre-coloured cloud turning to black over the desert, drifting eastwards—The chief of the armies fled that night—they had brought in crates of guinea pigs—they had the soldiers crawl across the Forward Zone—

The Reader's Digest Great World Atlas 1968

In the year of its second edition animals had cleaned the skeletons of the four dogs they shot and left in the bomb crater at Marcoo—where the family had camped on the still-warm earth, drinking black water—the child stillborn—and the black mist, greasy and thick, slid through Wallatinna and Mintabie and Ernabella, north of One Tree, Emu Field—In the year of its second edition in their secret Pearce report they declared Maralinga clean and signed a contract relieving their government of any further responsibility—they had ploughed more than twenty kilos of plutonium into the desert sand—a half-life of twenty-four thousand four hundred years—In the year of its second edition William Penney, 'father' of the Maralinga program, attended the House of Lords as a life peer, taking the title Baron Penney of East Hendred in the Royal County of Berkshire—At the Manhattan Project they had called him 'the smiling killer'—

In the year of its second edition Lake Karachay, having dried up, loosed its dust to the wind over the steppes, over half a million people—its lake bed, three-and-a-half metres of high-level radioactive dirt—In the year of its second edition the people of Enewetak sent a petition—'for twenty-two years the people of Enewetak have been living the life of exiles in our own country—these years have been hardship, poverty and near starvation'—the landing craft had arrived—the translator had said to them, 'You are like a rabbit fish wriggling on the end of a spear. You can struggle all you want, but there is nothing you can do to escape'—islands obliterated, plutonium in the lagoons, two-hundred megatons exploded over their Pacific Proving Grounds, radiated coral debris falling ankle-deep like snow—In the year of its second edition President Johnston promised the Bikinians they could return to their atoll—who had been exiled on Rongerik Atoll, on Kwajalein Atoll, on Kili Island, on Ejit—In the year of its second edition they said, 'There's virtually no radiation left and we can find no discernible effect on either plant or animal life'—the jellyfish babies, boneless, with transparent skin, the stillborn babies, their skin like a bunch of purple grapes—In the year of its second edition they exploded the plutonium bomb they called CHIC-8 over Lop Nur, on the Silk Road at the edge of the Tarim Basin, between the Taklamakan and Kumtag deserts in Xinjiang Province—where a potash mine is now—the site discovered on film from a KH-4 Corona 'national reconnaissance' satellite—In the year of its second edition they exploded the hydrogen bomb they called Canopus over Fangataufa Atoll—its cloud reached twenty-three thousand metres, drifting to the northeast, over Pukaroa, Tureia, Reao, the Gambier Islands—They classified their study of 'biological samples' the 'Service Mixte de Contrôle Biologique'—

The Reader's Digest Great World Atlas 1970

In the year of its third edition they exploded the bomb they called Dragon from a balloon over the Fregate Zone at Fangataufa Atoll near Moruroa—and Andromède, Cassiopée, Eridan, Licorne, Pégase, Orion, Toucan—the cloud widening over Moruroa, Tahiti, as far as Bora Bora—In the year of its third edition the people began moving back to Bikini Atoll—radiation in the pandanus, the coconuts, plutonium in the crater, a junkyard next to the village with more than twenty cubic metres of radiated debris—the child born there dying of cancer at eleven—In the year of its third edition they exploded the 3.4 megaton airdrop bomb they called CHIC-11 over Area D, Lop Nur—earth falling from the sky, without wind or storm, they watched it from the schoolyard—In the year of its third edition they exploded the nuclear bomb they called Baneberry underground at Yucca Flat on the Nevada Testing Site—its dust cloud, pouring upwards through a fissure, reached a height of three kilometres, raining on the workers, pluming out as far as California, as Washington—In the year of its third edition they announced their plan to explode the bomb they called Cannikin at Amchitka Island, midway in the arc of Alaska's Aleutian Islands—a five megaton bomb a mile deep under Cannikin lake, which, when it exploded, caused an earthquake, rockfalls, shock waves so strong they crushed the skulls of nearly a thousand sea otters, broke the spines of the birds—they had already excluded the Aleuts and Amchitka workers from their Radiation Exposure Compensation Act—In the year of its third edition they exploded nuclear bombs for craters—Holes 2-T and 6-T—on the Mangyshlak Plateau, east of the Caspian Sea—ostensibly for reservoirs of water, in what they called the 'Program for the Utilization of Nuclear Explosions in the National Economy'—In the year of its third edition they exploded sixteen underground bombs—in Semipalatinsk, in the frozen rock of Novaya Zemlya, at the Totskoye Testing Ground about a hundred kilometres east of the village of Totskoye, in the Orenburg Oblast, where once they had exploded the bomb they called 'Snowball' in the air over their troops—filming them marching out of their trenches, in the dust of the tanks, over the burning steppe—In the year of its third edition Ernest Titterton received his knighthood—He had said, 'If aboriginal people objected to the tests they would vote the government out'—

Landscape

A salt path leading back to the settlement—in through heaped coral rubble to the edge of the lagoon—Out of sight, the sea booms on the reef—white-grey sand by the concrete dome over the pit—To the north, light sheers off the ice, the glaciers grind and crack—The interior is mountainous—to the south the tundra is small shale, green algae on streaks of melting snow—here, where they saw, towards the end of winter, a mirage over the horizon—the sun a flattened hourglass shape, a floating rectangle—In the far distance a single tree, a ring of soft red dirt where nothing grows, littered with glass, beside a concrete plinth—Out from it, foot tracks enter into mile after mile of saltbush scrub, mallee, spinifex—the sandhills of the limestone plateau, north of the rail line, where the place of permanent water is hidden under the sand—In the dark, in the underground metro station, deserted, along the footpaths between the windowless apartments, towards a field of burnt-out planes and tanks, near where concrete towers rise out of the bare-earth mounds—From the hotel's picture window almost colourless grassland, shining in the long-angled light, widens out to a worn line of mountains darkening at the edges—The straight roads, the runway, a level plain pitted with craters, their smooth sheer walls of melted rock, by the blasted houses—Palm trees line the sand road passing by the deserted shacks to the strait where dark-winged birds mass—black branches behind the cyclone fence—or rifted mountains—Inland, its ruined stone huts, graves and brackish wells—its basalt slab roads lead across the island, past the freshwater lens, through small woods of catchbird trees, into the ocean—by the bay of wrecked ships, carriers, battleships, cruisers, destroyers, submarines, attack transports, landers—In the far distance—in its prohibited area—

Notes

Mirabilia

Some phrases are taken from Jan Huyghen van Linschoten's travel writing, Randall Jarrell's review of Elizabeth Bishop ('written underneath, "I have seen it"'), and Marianne Moore's letter to Ezra Pound ('could solve the problem of depicting a mind thinking so that the idea is not separate from the act of experiencing it').

The Replica (2020)

This poem was commissioned by David Ryding for the UNESCO City of Literature 'Melbourne Poets Laureate Poem of the Week' series during the coronavirus lockdown in Melbourne in 2020.

On the Characterisation of Male Poets' Mothers

This poem combines quotes from Wikipedia biographies of the poets and, sometimes, of their mothers.

The Book of Revelations

The poem's quotations come from Sidney Nolan's 1952 essay *Epic Drought in Australia* and from the Book of Revelations, *King James Version*. It was commissioned by Jessica Wilkinson for an anthology in response to Heide's 2021 *Modern Women* exhibition, curated by Chloe Jones.

Ekphrasis. The Nymph of Fontainebleau

This poem combines quotes from *The Autobiography of*

Benvenuto Cellini translated by John Addington Symonds (a translation adapted in places) and from the Louvre's descriptions of Mannerist art and of Cellini's *The Nymph of Fontainebleau.*

Tongue

In this part, the poems' quotations come from Leonardo da Vinci's *Notebooks*, translated by Jean Paul Richter, selected by Irma Richter, with an introduction and notes by Thereza Wells and preface by Martin Kemp (Oxford: Oxford University Press; 1952; 1908; 2008), and from the Book of Isaiah. The Lorenzo di Credi painting is his 'Madonna with the Christ Child and Saint John the Baptist' in the Gemäldegalerie, Dresden. These poems also include quotations from or allusions to Machiavelli's *Florentine Histories*, Poliziano's *History of the Pazzi Conspiracy*, Horace's 'Odes, I. xxxv', in Stephen de Vere's translation (*Temple Bar*, London, vol. 77, 1886), Ariosto's *Orlando Furioso*, Poliziano's *Stanze cominciate per la giostra del magnifico Giuliano di Pietro de Medici*, translated by David Quint in *The Stanze of Angelo Poliziano* (1979; 1993, the Pennsylvania State University Press), Robert Fagle's translation of *The Odyssey*, Plotinus's *Enneads*, Maurice Merleau-Ponty's *Themes from the Lectures,* translated by John O'Neill (Evanston, IL: Northwestern University Press, 1970), Benedetto Varchi's *Storia Fiorentina,* Castiglione's *Book of the Courtier*, Giorgio Vasari's *Lives of the Artists*, and the 1492 inventory of the Palazzo Medici, edited and translated by Richard Stapleford, *Lorenzo de' Medici At Home* (Pennsylvania State University Press, 2013). Among other sources, this poem draws on Alison Brown's biography of Bartolomeo Scala, *Bartolomeo Scala, 1430–1497, Chancellor of Florence: the Humanist as Bureaucrat* (Princeton Legacy Library, 1979; 2016), on Catherine Lawless's essay 'Women on the Margins: the "Beloved" and the "Mistress" in Renaissance Florence' in *Pawns or Players? Studies on Medieval and Early Modern Women*, ed. Christine Meek and Catherine Lawless (Dublin: Four Courts Press, 2003), on Linda Pellecchia's article 'The Patron's Role in the Production of Architecture: Bartolomeo Scala and the Scala Palace' (*Renaissance Quarterly*, Summer, 1989, vol. 42, no. 2, pp. 258–291), and on Lauro Martines's *April Blood: Florence and the Plot Against the Medici* (Oxford University Press, 2003).

It is only my surmise that Fioretta (Antonia del Ciptadino, or Cittadino) was the model for Leonardo da Vinci's 'Madonna of the Flowers', also known as the Benois Madonna – one of two paintings of the Virgin Mary which Leonardo began in the year of the Pazzi Conspiracy, the other being the 'Madonna of the Carnation'. Fioretta's child Giulio de' Medici became Pope Clement VII. At some point, according to Vasari, Leonardo gave his painting of the 'Madonna of the Carnation' to Giulio de' Medici. It is only my surmise that Leonardo might also have given Giulio de' Medici his 'Madonna of the Flowers'; also, only my surmise that the flowers in those two paintings might have been suggested by Fioretta's name.

It is also only my surmise that Verrocchio and da Vinci made the copper-gilt sallet in the shape of a lion's head for the giostra of Giuliano de' Medici. The sallet is in the Metropolitan Museum of Art and visible here: <https://www.metmuseum.org/art/collection/search/22860>.

The name of Giulio de' Medici's mother is typically given as Fioretta Gorini – but Varchi says that this was a lie the Medici invented, as they invented the fiction that Giulio de' Medici's parents had married in a secret ceremony before Giulio was born.

Great World Atlas

These poems were commissioned by Izabela Pluta and first published (in slightly different form) in Pluta's artist's book *Figures of slippage and oscillation* (Perimeter Editions, 2019), 'drawing on a series of darkroom contact prints titled *Spatial misalignments*, conceived by shining light through the pages of three long-out-of print editions of the *Reader's Digest Great World Atlas*' (<perimeterbooks.com>).

Acknowledgements

I am grateful to the curators and editors of publications in which earlier versions of these poems appeared: David McCooey and Australian Poetry CEO Jacinta Le Plastrier, *Australian Poetry 10.1, Modern Elegy* (2020) for 'Mirabilia'; John Kinsella and Jacinta Le Plastrier in *Australian Poetry 9.1 resist* (2019) for 'Ekphrasis. The Nymph of Fontainebleau'; Peter Rose, John Hawke and Judith Bishop of *Australian Book Review* (May 2020 no. 421) for 'On the Characterisation of Male Poets' Mothers'; Jessica Wilkinson, 'Rabbit Poet Series / Heide Modern Women: House of Ideas' (2021) for 'The Book of Revelations'; David Ryding of the 'Melbourne Poets Laureate Poem of the Week' series in Melbourne for 'Replica'; and John Kinsella and Kent MacCarter of *Cordite 101: No Theme 10* for one part of 'Great World Atlas'. I am grateful to Izabela Pluta for commissioning the poems in 'Great World Atlas', which were first published in her artist's book *Figures of Slippage and Oscillation* (Perimeter Press, 2019), and I thank Justine Ellis and Dan Rule of Perimeter Press for their care in setting out the poems in that publication.

I am grateful to Ivor Indyk and Evelyn Juers of Giramondo for longstanding support, and thank Aleesha Paz for her astute editorial work. My warmest thanks to John, Kelso, Toby and Penelope Wentworth for their encouragement. This collection is dedicated to my mother Sue Gorton, in gratitude.

These poems were written on the traditional lands of the Wurundjeri people of the Kulin nation and the author respectfully acknowledges their Elders past, present and future.

About the author

Lisa Gorton is a poet, novelist, and essayist. She lives in Melbourne. Lisa completed a doctorate on John Donne's poetry and prose at Oxford University. Her awards include the Philip Hodgins Memorial Medal, the Victorian Premier's Prize for Poetry, the Vincent Buckley Poetry Prize, the NSW Premier's People's Choice Award for Fiction, and the Prime Minister's Prize for Fiction (shared). *Mirabilia* is her fourth poetry collection.